MW01042834

ONE NATION

Chinese Americans

Nichol Bryan

ABDO
Publishing Company

visit us at
www.abdopub.com

Published by ABDO Publishing Company, 4940 Viking Drive, Edina, Minnesota 55435. Copyright © 2004 by Abdo Consulting Group, Inc. International copyrights reserved in all countries. No part of this book may be reproduced in any form without written permission from the publisher.

Printed in the United States.

Cover Photo: Corbis
Interior Photos: Corbis pp. 1, 2-3, 5, 7, 8, 10, 11, 14, 15, 17, 18, 19, 20, 21, 23, 24, 25, 27, 28, 29, 30-31

Series Coordinator: Jennifer R. Krueger
Editors: Kristianne E. Buechler, Kate A. Conley
Art Direction & Maps: Neil Klinepier

All of the U.S. population statistics in the One Nation series are taken from the 2000 Census.

Library of Congress Cataloging-in-Publication Data

Bryan, Nichol, 1958-
      Chinese Americans / Nichol Bryan.
           p. cm. -- (One nation)
      Includes index.
      Summary: Provides information on the history of China and on the customs, language,
religion, and experiences of Chinese Americans.
      ISBN 1-59197-525-5
      1. Chinese Americans--Juvenile literature. [1. Chinese Americans. 2. Immigrants.] I. Title.

E184.C5B79 2004
973'.04951--dc21

                                                                                    2003056264

Contents

Chinese Americans

Christopher Columbus, an Italian explorer working for Spain, traveled to the New World in 1492. This set off a wave of exploration by Europeans. People from England, France, Spain, and the Netherlands came to start colonies in the Americas.

In the 1800s and 1900s, groups of **immigrants** from all over the world came to American shores. Many of these immigrants came from China. Some were looking for freedom and opportunity. Others wished to escape poverty and war. Most wanted to earn a living that would support their families.

New Americans are still coming from all over the world. Throughout America's history, immigrants have faced **discrimination** and injustice. They have struggled to learn a new language and a new way of life. Through their struggles, they have taught everyone what it means to be American.

Opposite page: *Members of the Chinese Community Girls Drill Team at a parade in Seattle, Washington*

An Ancient Land

China is the only ancient civilization that still exists today. For thousands of years, this land was ruled by a series of dynasties. The kings of these dynasties were actually rulers of separate states. In AD 221, the states were unified into one empire, and the kings were called emperors.

Under the emperors, China became a powerful country. Other nations were eager to trade with China for its silks, spices, and teas. By trading with other nations, China became an important part of the world.

But throughout China's history, outsiders have threatened its borders. After losing wars against Japan and Britain in the late 1800s, China was forced to give up the territories of Hong Kong and Taiwan. Some Chinese resented the impact of Westerners on their country. So, they rose up against foreigners in the Boxer Rebellion.

China struggled with other conflicts within the country. In 1911, revolutionaries who wanted China to be a **republic** overthrew the

The Great Wall of China was built to protect the country from invasions.

emperor. They later formed the Nationalist Party. This began a struggle between the Nationalists and the **Communists** for control of China. Mao Tse-tung led the Chinese Communist Party.

During this struggle, Japan invaded China. By the end of **World War II**, Japan controlled large portions of China. This continued until the **Allies**, including China, defeated Japan in 1945. But, the defeat of the Japanese did not bring peace to China.

An artist paints a portrait of Mao Tse-tung.

A civil war continued between the Nationalists and the **Communists**. Mao Tse-tung defeated the Nationalists, who retreated to the island of Taiwan. Many people who come from Taiwan still consider themselves to be Chinese, however. In 1949, Mao declared the creation of the People's **Republic** of China.

Mao had many ideas about how to improve the country's industry and agriculture. Industry grew quickly under his plans, but Mao's ideas on agriculture were less successful. They eventually led to food shortages and a **depression**.

Moreover, the communist government harshly punished anyone who disagreed with its policies. Mao died in 1976, but Communists continue to rule the government. The Chinese government has killed or imprisoned many who asked for more freedoms in China. Despite this, the people do have more freedom than in the past.

Throughout China's history, its people have faced hardships. So beginning in the mid-1800s, some Chinese started to move to the United States. They were trying to get away from the wars, food shortages, and political troubles. Today, many Chinese still come to America in search of a better life for themselves and their families.

The Journey from China to the United States

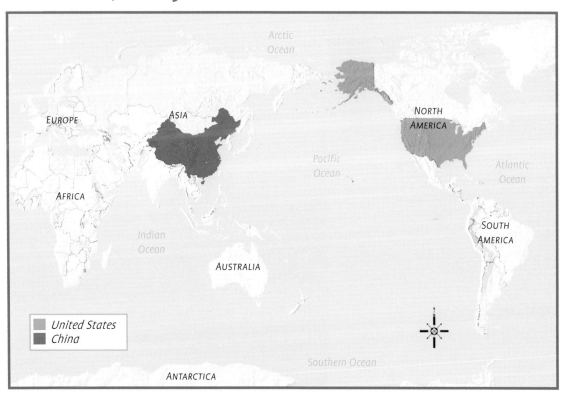

Gold Mountain

Although they were a world away, China and America did business with each other, even in colonial times. Goods such as silk and tea from China were traded with America. In fact, the tea dumped into Boston Harbor during the famous **Boston Tea Party** came from China!

Lured by the discovery of gold, the Chinese began coming to California in the 1840s. Even the Chinese name for America, *Gum Saan*, means "Gold Mountain." But, the Chinese found more hardship than wealth in the California gold rush.

Many Chinese Americans found only dangerous jobs in the United States, such as working on railroads.

More Chinese came to America in the 1860s to work on the Central Pacific Railroad. This was part of the first railroad across North America. Thousands of Chinese workers did the hardest and most dangerous labor. They broke rocks and planted explosives to blast holes through the mountains. Hundreds of Chinese workers died.

A camp of Chinese workers building the Central Pacific Railroad

Many stayed in the country after the completion of the railroad. They became merchants, workers, or farmers. However, they usually earned money working for others, rather than owning their own businesses or farms.

In 1882, the U.S. government severely restricted Chinese **immigration**. Congress passed the Chinese Exclusion Act. This law kept Chinese laborers from entering the country. The act was renewed after its ten-year time limit was up.

The United States would not open again to Chinese immigration until 1943. That year, Congress withdrew the Chinese Exclusion Act. Chinese immigrants could at last become U.S. citizens. Many settled in California and Washington. But today, Chinese Americans live all over the country.

Chinese still come to America. Some come to study or work for a short time, but others stay permanently. Some come to seek political protection from China's **communist** government. In 2000, there were almost 2.5 million Chinese Americans.

Today, many Chinese Americans have college degrees. Because of this, they may have high-paying management, professional, or technical jobs. They are more likely to live where more of these jobs are available. So, many Chinese Americans live in cities rather than in small towns or in the country.

Chinese-American Communities

Legend:
- More than 500,000 Chinese Americans
- Between 100,000 and 500,000 Chinese Americans
- Between 25,000 and 100,000 Chinese Americans
- Between 5,000 and 25,000 Chinese Americans
- Between 1,000 and 5,000 Chinese Americans
- Fewer than 1,000 Chinese Americans

Challenges

Chinese Americans faced **discrimination** in the United States. They were looked down upon. This was because they looked different and had different lifestyles from other Americans. They also lived in tightly knit groups in communities called Chinatowns. They were kept out of most jobs. And, they were sometimes violently attacked.

Chinese Americans also struggled because they were not U.S. citizens. Because of this, they often had their property seized or were driven away from farms or mines. Many Chinese men who came to America could not make enough money to take back to their families in China. These men made a hard living by operating laundries, something they had never done in their homeland.

Chinese Americans read about Japan's surrender in World War II.

But despite the hostility of their new home, Chinese Americans gradually adapted to their new **culture**. After **World War I**, Chinese Americans who had served in the army earned the right to become U.S. citizens. Chinese Americans won new respect through their military service in World War I and **World War II**.

During World War II, these Chinese Americans helped the war effort by working at a shipbuilding yard in New Jersey.

Becoming a Citizen

The Chinese and other **immigrants** who come to the United States take the same path to citizenship. Immigrants become citizens in a process called naturalization. A government agency called the United States Citizenship and Immigration Services (USCIS) oversees this process.

The Path to Citizenship

Applying for Citizenship

The first step in becoming a citizen is filling out a form. It is called the Application for Naturalization. On the application, immigrants provide information about their past. Immigrants send the application to the USCIS.

Providing Information

Besides the application, immigrants must provide the USCIS with other items. They may include documents such as marriage licenses or old tax returns. Immigrants must also provide photographs and fingerprints. They are used for identification. The fingerprints are also used to check whether immigrants have committed crimes in the past.

The Interview

Next, a USCIS officer interviews each immigrant to discuss his or her application and background. In addition, the USCIS officer tests the immigrant's ability to speak, read, and write in English. The officer also tests the immigrant's knowledge of American civics.

The Oath

Immigrants approved for citizenship must take the Oath of Allegiance. Once immigrants take this oath, they are citizens. During the oath, immigrants promise to renounce loyalty to their native country, to support the U.S. Constitution, and to serve and defend the United States when needed.

Sample Questions from the Civics Test

How many stars are there on our flag?

What is the capital of the state you live in?

Why did the Pilgrims come to America?

How many senators are there in Congress?

Who said, "Give me liberty or give me death"?

What are the first 10 amendments to the Constitution called?

In what month do we vote for the president?

Why Become a Citizen?

Why would an immigrant want to become a U.S. citizen? There are many reasons. Perhaps the biggest reason is that the U.S. Constitution grants many rights to its citizens. One of the most important is the right to vote.

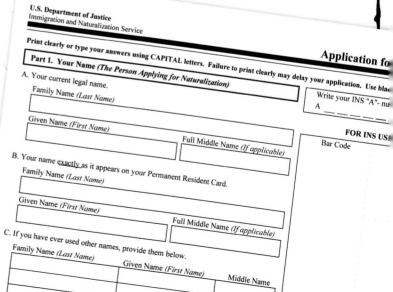

U.S. Department of Justice
Immigration and Naturalization Service

Print clearly or type your answers using CAPITAL letters. Failure to print clearly may delay your application. Use blac

Application fo

Part 1. Your Name *(The Person Applying for Naturalization)*

A. Your current legal name.

Family Name *(Last Name)*

Given Name *(First Name)*

Full Middle Name *(If applicable)*

Write your INS "A"- nu
A _ _ _ _ _ _ _ _

FOR INS US

Bar Code

B. Your name <u>exactly</u> as it appears on your Permanent Resident Card.

Family Name *(Last Name)*

Given Name *(First Name)*

Full Middle Name *(If applicable)*

C. If you have ever used other names, provide them below.

Family Name *(Last Name)*

Given Name *(First Name)*

Middle Name

Ancient Culture

The Chinese have strong traditions that date back thousands of years. Chinese **immigrants** brought these traditions with them to America. Chinese Americans share a **culture** rich with family, celebrations, food, religion, and language.

Family Is Strength

For the Chinese, their place in the family is a large part of who they are. Traditionally, Chinese live in extended families. When a woman gets married, she is expected to live with her husband's parents. These families pool all their money and property. The elder men of the family make the financial decisions.

Some Chinese Americans adapt to having more Western-style families. But, many Chinese cultural traditions still live on.

A Chinese-American family in San Francisco celebrates the New Year together.

Celebrating the Seasons

One of the most important Chinese holidays is the Lunar New Year, which is usually celebrated in February. The Chinese traditionally clean their homes and buy new clothing during this holiday. Many cities with large Chinese-American populations have major New Year's parades. These include long dragon floats dancing down the street.

Another seasonal holiday, the Moon Festival, is held in autumn. It's a time for families and friends to get together under the light of the full moon. They celebrate with mooncakes, which are pastries filled with lotus seed paste.

A Chinese New Year celebration in Los Angeles, California

The Way of the Wok

Chinese food is a favorite of people all over the world. At first, Chinese **immigrants** started restaurants in Chinatowns to provide familiar meals to others from China. But, other Americans soon discovered these restaurants as well. People loved the flavors of Chinese cooking. Today, most American towns have at least one Chinese restaurant.

Chinese cooking features a wide variety of ingredients, including beef, chicken, pork, shrimp, lobster, and all kinds of vegetables. Chinese food is often cooked in a wok, a large pan with sloping sides. A Chinese cook usually cuts food into bite-sized pieces before it is cooked. That way it can easily be eaten with chopsticks.

Many Chinese dishes include vegetables, meat, and rice.

Plates of Chinese food

Ancient Beliefs

The Chinese who first came to America held many religious beliefs. Many of them were Taoist. *Tao* is a word meaning "way," or "road." In Taoism, the Tao is the force behind nature and reality. Taoists try to be in harmony with the Tao through the study of nature. Many Chinese Americans still practice Taoism.

Chinese Americans hold other beliefs as well. Many honor the teachings of Confucius, a wise man who lived 2,500 years ago. He taught that people must respect wisdom, virtue, and tradition. He also taught that people must honor their parents, as well as their departed ancestors.

Many Chinese are also Buddhists. Buddhism is based on the teachings of Siddhartha Gautama. He was called Buddha, or "enlightened one." Buddhists try to let go of greed and to follow Buddha's teachings. Buddhists hope to reach nirvana, which means a carefree state or oneness with the universe.

A new religious movement in China is *falun gong*. It has many followers in China, the United States, and around the world. This movement encourages people to live healthy, moral lives, to practice meditation, and to exercise.

A Buddhist temple in
New York's Chinatown

A Musical Language

Chinese can be difficult for Americans to master because of its unfamiliar characters.

Would you like to learn a language that has the most native speakers on Earth? Then learn Chinese! Chinese has been the language of poets and scholars for thousands of years. But, Chinese is very different from Western languages such as Spanish, French, or English.

For example, in Chinese, almost all words have just one **syllable**. The meaning of a word depends on the tone of the speaker's voice. And, Chinese does not have an alphabet the way Western languages do. Instead, it has a symbol for each idea or thing.

Chinese who come to America often like to live among other Chinese speakers. But, learning English helps Chinese **immigrants** do well in school and at work. English is taught in many schools in China. So, many immigrants arrive in the United States already knowing the language. The children of Chinese immigrants also learn English when they start attending American schools.

This Chinese character means "tea"

Achievements

Chinese Americans are heirs to a history of achievement in the arts and sciences. So, it's no wonder that many of America's most notable artists, musicians, scientists, and mathematicians have Chinese ancestors.

A Chinese American created one of the most popular monuments in Washington, D.C. Maya Lin designed the Vietnam Veterans Memorial. The names of the Americans who died in the **Vietnam War** are carved on the wall. The wall has brought comfort to millions of Americans.

One of the most famous Chinese Americans comes from the music world. Cello player Yo-Yo Ma was an outstanding musician even as a small boy. He was giving public recitals by the age of five! Since then, Ma has recorded more than 50 albums and has won 14 Grammy Awards.

Yo-Yo Ma

Chinese Americans have also become best-selling authors. You may have read books by Laurence Yep. His popular books for young readers include the Golden Mountain Chronicles and the Chinatown Mystery series. Two of Yep's books have won the Newbery Honor Award for children's books.

Many inventors of advanced technology have also been Chinese American. He may not be a household name, but Steve Chen is one of these influential inventors. Born in Taiwan, Steve Chen moved to the United States and pioneered the design of very large, fast

computers. He holds more than 35 patents for his computer inventions.

One of the most famous Chinese Americans has made her name in sports. Michelle Kwan has won the World Figure Skating Championship five

Steve Chen

times. Many Americans eagerly watched Kwan's performance at the 2002 Winter Olympic Games in Salt Lake City, Utah, where she won a bronze medal.

Chinese Americans have overcome more than a century of **discrimination**. Today, they are gaining recognition as one of America's most accomplished ethnic groups. Through hard work and determination, they have made America a better place for everyone.

Michelle Kwan has earned 37 perfect 6.0 scores in major competitions, more than any other skater in history!

Glossary

allies - people or countries that agree to help each other in times of need. During World War II, Great Britain, France, China, the United States, and the Soviet Union were called the Allies.

Boston Tea Party - December 16, 1773. About 60 Boston colonists, dressed as Native Americans, boarded a ship in Boston Harbor. They threw a shipment of tea overboard to protest the Stamp Act of 1765.

Communism - a social and economic system in which everything is owned by the government and is distributed to the people as needed.

culture - the customs, arts, and tools of a nation or people at a certain time.

depression - a period of economic trouble when there is little buying or selling and many people are out of work.

discrimination - unfair treatment based on factors such as a person's race, religion, or gender.

immigration - entry into another country to live. People who immigrate are called immigrants.

republic - a form of government in which authority rests with voting citizens and is carried out by elected officials, such as those in a parliament.

syllable - a single, uninterrupted sound.

Vietnam War - from 1957 to 1975. A long, failed attempt by the United States to stop North Vietnam from taking over South Vietnam.

World War I - from 1914 to 1918, fought in Europe. The United States, Great Britain, France, Russia, and their allies were on one side. Germany, Austria-Hungary, and their allies were on the other side.

World War II - from 1939 to 1945, fought in Europe, Asia, and Africa. The United States, France, Great Britain, the Soviet Union, and their allies were on one side. Germany, Italy, Japan, and their allies were on the other side.

Saying It

Confucius - kuhn-FYOO-shuhs
Gum Saan - GUM SAHN
Mao Tse-tung - MOWD-ZUH-DUHNG
Siddhartha Gautama - sihd-DAHR-tuh GOW-tuh-muh
Taiwan - TIE-WAHN
Tao - DOW

Web Sites

To learn more about Chinese Americans, visit ABDO Publishing
Company on the World Wide Web at **www.abdopub.com**. Web sites
about Chinese Americans are featured on our Book Links page. These
links are routinely monitored and updated to provide the most
current information available.

Index